# LEARNING TO **LISTEN**

*Making sense of spoken English*

## Lin Lougheed

Student Book 2

MACMILLAN

Macmillan Education
Between Towns Road, Oxford OX4 3PP
A division of Macmillan Publishers Limited
Companies and representatives throughout the world

ISBN 0 333 98888 4

First published 2003

Designed by Xen Media Ltd
Illustrated by Kevin Hopgood, Louise Morgan, Val Saunders
and Jane Smith
Cover design by Xen Media Ltd
Cover illustration by Coneyl Jay

The publishers would like to thank Hiroshi Asano, Stuart
Bowie, James Boyd, Anthony Brewer, David Brooks, Steven R.
Brownell, Sylvia Chao, Frank Claypool, Elizabeth E. Colford,
Peter Collins, Sheelagh Conway, Ann Cunningham, Janet
Denny, Joseph Dias, Gary Farmer, Clyde Fowle, Masaki
Fujimoto, William Green, Takashi Hata, Grace Hsu, Yukari
Kanzaki, Yuko Kobayashi, Jeong Sook Lee, Mallory Leece,
Pearl Lin, Peter Littlewood, Terry McKinnon, Steve Maginn,
Richard Manuel, Charlene Mills, Harumi Nakazawa, James
Pagel, Tawatchai Pattarawongvisut, John Perkins, Harumi
Nakazawa, Rube Redfield, Cristina Roberts, Terry Roberts,
Elizabeth Root, Satoshi Saito, Yoshiharu Saito, Maria Luiza
Santos, Hajime Shishido, Elliot Taback, Tadakuni Tajiri,
Andrew Todd, Kris Vicca, Genet Falconeri Watanabe, David
Wade, Robert Weschler, Sandra Wu

The authors and publishers would like to thank the following
for permission to reproduce their photographs: Alamy/
C.Fredriksson p50(d); Anthony Blake pp 37(1), 37(2);
Corbis/FK.Photo p9(a), J.Rogers p27(a), Stockmarket p67(a),
R.McMahon p71; Getty/Yellow Dog Production p9(b),
K.Thatcher p9(c), C.Harvey p9(d), Real Life p18(b), J.Tisne
p19, R.Lockyer p23(1), Getty/Taxi p25(2), P.Edmondson p27(b),
D.Smetzer p27(c), S.Stickler p39, D de Lossy p43(1), 43(3),
E.O'Connell p43(2), J.Silva Production p43(4), M.Romanelli
p49(l), P.Fiqura p49(r), S.Weinberg p50(a), S.Cohen p50(b),
S.Achernar p50(c), G.Buss p67(2), S.Smith p67(d),
M.Krasowitz p69(1), D.Paul Production p69(2), C.Wilhelm
p73(1), D.Rosenberg p73(2), E.Dooley p75; ImageState pp
18(a), 18(c), 18(d), 67(c); NASA p14; Powerstock pp 25(1),
27(d); Science Photo Library/A. Bartel p23(2).

Printed and bound in Thailand

2007 2006 2005
10 9 8 7 6 5 4

# Contents

# Scope and Sequence

| Unit | | Topic | Skills |
|---|---|---|---|
| 1 | Born Lucky | Describing personalities and personality traits Talking about your friends | Identifying characteristics and habits Identifying an opinion Distinguishing between different sentence intonations |
| 2 | Around the World | Learning about countries, languages, and nationalities | Identifying names of countries, languages, and nationalities Distinguishing the stressed syllable in a word |
| 3 | Happy Birthday | Celebrating birthdays Dates, invitations, gifts | Identifying invitations Identifying an opinion Distinguishing ordinal and cardinal numbers |
| 4 | How Are You Feeling? | Talking about health problems and remedies | Identifying health problems Distinguishing the number of syllables in a word |

Review 1

| Unit | | Topic | Skills |
|---|---|---|---|
| 5 | At the Mall | Spending time at the mall | Identifying types of stores Identifying direction and location Distinguishing the pronunciation of regular past tense verbs |
| 6 | At the Movies | Talking about movies | Identifying different features of movies Identifying likes and dislikes Distinguishing stressed words in sentences |
| 7 | Dining Out | Eating at restaurants Describing different food | Identifying preferences Identifying location Identifying time Distinguishing between different ways of expressing amounts of money |
| 8 | What Are You Wearing? | Describing clothes | Identifying clothes Identifying opinion and advice Distinguishing between /s/, /z/, and /ɪz/ in plural nouns |

4

# Introduction to the Student

This series will help you become more confident about the listening you do both inside and outside the classroom.

With these books you will:
- learn to listen appropriately
- learn to understand correctly
- learn to make more sense of what you hear.

You will hear a variety of sources such as conversations, messages, radio broadcasts, and other forms of real English, and you will learn to listen both for detail and for the general meaning.

As students you want to feel confident in real-life situations when you are speaking English. Through this series you will hear what real English speakers say in everyday situations, such as meeting strangers or planning a celebration, and learn to understand the words they use.

This series prepares you to react appropriately to the people you meet by helping you to make sense of the meaning behind the words they use. You will learn about the influences of a speaker's mood, location, and background on the language she or he uses.

You will gain confidence in listening and responding to everyday situations in English. You'll be able to react to the personalities of the people you meet, understand the words they use, and make sense of what you hear.

# Introduction to the Teacher

This three-book listening series helps make every minute of the classroom experience as rich as the real world. The topics, the activities, the personalities, the beliefs, and the accents reflect the variety in the world around us. In the series, students meet different people, discuss different things, have different attitudes, and have different reactions.

To make the listening experience as authentic as possible, the series presents listening challenges from a variety of sources: dialogs, recorded messages, monologues, radio broadcasts, reviews, public service announcements, and weather announcements.

In these books students tackle real-world tasks that prepare them for the kind of listening they will do outside the classroom: listening for different purposes, making inferences, personalizing the experience, and making assumptions and predictions.

Students need to be actively involved in the process of learning to listen and listening to learn, because this makes learning much more effective. This is achieved by asking them to listen for a purpose, read the clues about speakers' mood, intention and background, and making students aware of the process they use in their own native language to make linguistic input comprehensible.

Students wish to react and express themselves appropriately in real-life situations. For that reason, all three books show how people react and cope in everyday situations – and they do so in a way that shows their personality, character, and attitude. By listening to, observing, and judging people in these contexts, students will learn that they too are able to express their personality when they speak English – a major step in becoming proficient in English.

# 1 Born Lucky

1979  1980  1981
1982  1983  1984

## 1 What's going on?

**Look at the picture and complete the chart.**

| Person | Born | Sign | Character |
|--------|------|------|-----------|
| Charles | | | creative, romantic |
| Sandra | | | intelligent, practical |
| Tom | | | wants to be successful, generous |
| Mark | 1982 | | a true friend, not selfish |
| Dale | | Monkey | friendly, loves to talk |
| Lee Ann | | | positive, fun |

## 2 What's your character?

**Listen and number the Chinese signs.**

a. ☐ Pig     c. ☐ Sheep     e. ☐ Monkey
b. ☐ Rooster     d. ☐ Rat     f. ☐ Dog

**3** What's your sign?

**Listen and circle the correct Chinese sign. Then listen again and write the year of birth.**

1. (Rat)/ Pig  *very intelligent*    Year of birth: 1972.
2. Sheep / Pig    Year of birth: 1971.
3. Rat / Sheep  *friendly*    Year of birth: 1979.
4. (Dog)/ Monkey  *but selfish  not very smart*    Year of birth: 1970

*I've friend  but  generous  honest*

**4** Do you think I'm smart?

**Listen and number the pictures. Then listen again and match the speaker's trait with the picture.**

a.

c.

b.

d.

☐3 Generous     ☐2 Romantic     ☐4 Intelligent     ☐1 Funny

Train your ear

When we ask questions, we don't always use words such as *when, what, who, do, did.* Sometimes we use intonation to change a statement to a question.

A statement has falling intonation:    A question has rising intonation:
*Mary was born in 1982.*        *Mary was born in 1982?*

**Listen and put a question mark (?) or a period (.) at the end of each sentence.**

1. Mark's a Sheep ___
2. Dale's a Monkey ___
3. Hiro is honest and generous ___

4. She's generous ___
5. Sandra was born in 1984 ___
6. He's friendly and romantic ___

**6** Opposites attract

**Listen and write if the people are the same (S) or different (D). Then listen again and write the missing word.**

1. ⬚   2. D   3. ⬚   4. D   5. ⬚   6. S

a. Well, I'm _quiet & shy_ .
b. And I like to be with _major_ .

c. You're too _generous_ .
d. Give me my _money_ back.

e. You make me _laugh_ .
f. We're just _alike_ !

g. I think things will turn out _okay_ .
h. I'm _positive_ , but not stupid.

i. Try to be more _outgoing_ .
j. They don't _know_ you.

k. I'm not interested in _success_ at all.
l. I'm not _lazy_ .

lazy
generous
badly
people
outgoing
laugh
quiet
know
money
alike
positive
success

**Test yourself**

**Listen and circle the answer that matches the picture.**

1. (A) (B) (C)                    2. (A) (B) (C)

**Listen and circle the best response.**

3. (A) (B) (C)                    4. (A) (B) (C)

**Listen to the conversation and to the question that follows. Circle the best answer.**

5. (A) Dog.                       6. (A) They're both positive.
   (B) Sheep.                        (B) They're both opposites.
   (C) Pig.                          (C) They're both alike.

**8** **Your turn**

Write your personal information. Then ask two people for their information. Are you the same or different? Use: *When were you born? What are three of your characteristics? What are three of your friend's characteristics?*

|  | You | Person 1 | Person 2 |
| --- | --- | --- | --- |
| Date of birth |  |  |  |
| Characteristics | 1 | 1 | 1 |
|  | 2 | 2 | 2 |
|  | 3 | 3 | 3 |
| Friends' characteristics | 1 | 1 | 1 |
|  | 2 | 2 | 2 |
|  | 3 | 3 | 3 |

# 2 Around the World

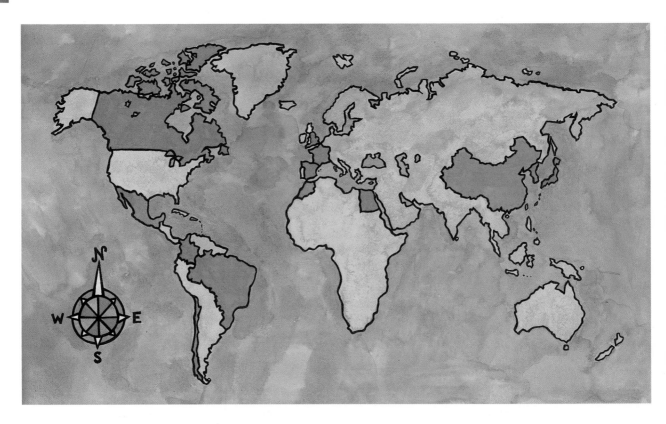

## 1 What's going on?

**Put the number of the country on the map. Then write the correct nationality next to each country.**

1. Mexico — Mexican
2. Chile — South of Columbia (Portugal)
3. England —
4. France —
5. Spain — arabic/egypt
6. Colombia —
7. Brazil — Spanish — south of united states

8. China — east of china/west of japan
9. Japan —
10. Korea —
11. Morocco — (not near france)
12. Egypt —
13. Canada —

## 2 Which country?

**Listen and circle the correct country.**

1. Morocco / Portugal
2. Brazil / Mexico
3. China / Korea

4. Brazil / Portugal
5. Egypt / Morocco

**3** Where are you from?

Listen and circle the correct country in columns 1 and 2. Then listen again and in column 3 circle the language they speak.

|  | From ... | Now lives in ... | Speaks ... |
|---|---|---|---|
| 1. | Spain / Colombia | (Spain) / Colombia | (Spanish) / Portuguese / Arabic |
| 2. | (Portugal) / France | Portugal / (France) | Spanish / (French) / Portuguese |
| 3. | (Morocco) / Japan | Morocco / (Japan) | Arabic / French / (Japanese) |
| 4. | China / (England) | (China) / England | Korean / Japanese / (Chinese) |

**4** Where did you go?

Listen and number the maps. Then listen again and check (✓) the country or countries that each person visited.

a.
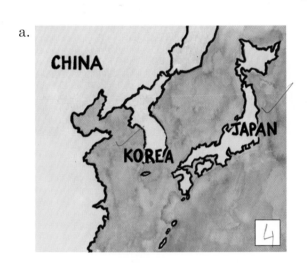

b.
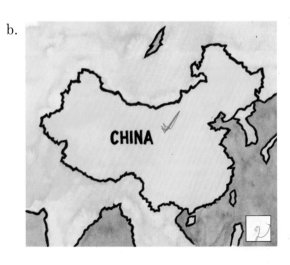

c.
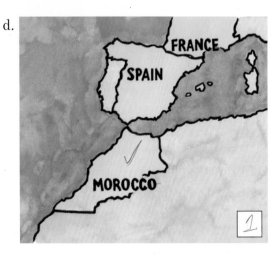

d.

13

## 5 Train your ear

**When words have more than one syllable, one of the syllables is stressed. Listen to the examples:**

● ● ●    ● ● ●    ● ● ● ●

*Mex-i-co    Mo-roc-co    E-gyp-tian*

**Now listen and draw a dot (•) over the syllable that is stressed in each word.**

1. Ja-pan
2. Ja-pa-nese
3. Chi-na
4. Chi-nese
5. Co-lom-bia
6. Co-lom-bian
7. Ko-re-a
8. Ko-re-an
9. na-tion
10. na-tion-a-li-ty

## 6 Any place is fine

**Listen and circle the noun or adjective.**

|   | Noun | Adjective |
|---|------|-----------|
| 1. | France | / French |
| 2. | China | / Chinese |
| 3. | Korea | / Korean |

|   | Noun | Adjective |
|---|------|-----------|
| 4. | Egypt | / Egyptian |
| 5. | Mexico | / Mexican |

Test yourself

**Listen and circle the answer that matches the picture.**

1. (A) (B) (C)                    2.  (A) (B) (C)

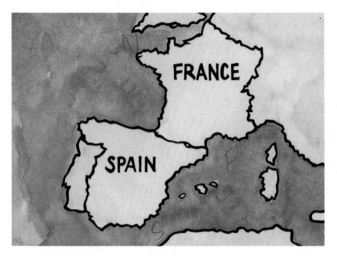

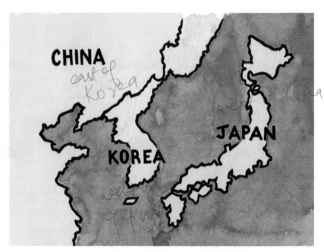

**Listen and circle the best response.**

3. (A) (B) (C)                    4. (A) (B) (C)

**Listen to the conversation and to the question that follows.
Circle the best answer.**

5. (A) Egyptian.                  6.  (A) He's Mexican.
   (B) Japanese.                     (B) He's Spanish.
   (C) Chinese.                      (C) He's Canadian.

Your turn

Use the map in Activity 1. Choose a country. Give your
partner clues, one at a time, and ask your partner to guess
the name of the country. Use: *It's north of Mexico. The people
there speak English and some people speak Spanish. There are
about 300 million people.*

Country X

# 3 Happy Birthday

## 1 What's going on?

**Circle the activities you see in the picture. What do you do to celebrate your birthday? Add some activities to the list.**

1. sing *Happy Birthday*
2. blow out candles
3. give presents
4. decorate with balloons
5. dance
6. wear birthday hats
7. eat ice cream
8. eat cake
9. play games
10. _____
11. _____

## 2 What do you do?

**Listen and number the events in the order they happen.**

|    | Sing Happy Birthday | Blow out candles | Open presents | Dance | Eat cake |
|----|---------------------|------------------|---------------|-------|----------|
| a. | 3 | 4 | 1 | 2 | 5 |
| b. | 1 | 2 | 4 | 5 | 3 |
| c. |   |   |   |   |   |
| d. |   |   |   |   |   |

## 3 Train your ear

**When spoken, some ordinal numbers can be confused. Listen to the example:**

*It's my ninetieth birthday. It's my birthday on the nineteenth.*

**Listen to people talk about their birthdays and circle the correct number.**

1. 16th / 60th
2. 4th / 14th

3. 15th / 50th
4. 17th / 70th

## 4 You shouldn't have

**Listen and check (✓) what the person received.**

1.

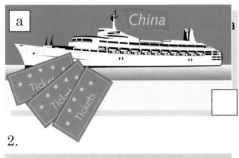

2.

3.

4.

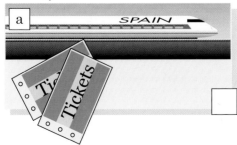

## 5 Can you come to my party?

**Listen and number the invitations. Then listen again and write the missing information.**

a.

# Martha's 18!

Please celebrate this special occasion with us.

Saturday the __18th__ at __8:30pm__

Hope to see you there.

`4`

c.

# It's Krishna's Birthday.

You're invited for dinner and __dancing__.

Saturday the __28th__ at __8pm__.

Bring your hottest __CDs__

`2`

b.

## Come celebrate 80 years with Jane.

When: Saturday the __18th__

What time: __3pm__

Where: Maria's Café

Bring __balloons__ (and a big appetite!)

`3`

d.

Dear Jimmy **I`m 8!**

Please come to my birthday party on Saturday the __22nd__ at __3pm__

Tommy

P.S: We'll have cake and __games__!

Mom says no presents, but don't listen to her.

`1`

## 6 Who's coming?

**Listen and check (✓) if the guests are coming or not. Then listen again and correct any mistakes on the list.**

| | Guest | Coming | Not coming |
|---|---|---|---|
| 1. | Tina Campos | ✓ | |
| 2. | Greg Hew | ✓ | |
| 3. | Burt Ward | ✓ | |
| 4. | Paco Ramirez | | ✓ |
| 5. | Maria López | ✓ | |
| 6. | Jane Dwyer | ✓ | |
| 7. | S. Grant | ✓ | |
| 8. | D. Brant | | ✓ |

Listen and circle the answer that matches the picture.

1. (A) (B) (C)    2. (A) (B) (C)

Come to my party,
Saturday the 15th at 5:00

Listen and circle the best response.

3. (A) (B) (C)    4. (A) (B) (C)

Listen to the conversation and to the question that follows.
Circle the best answer.

5. (A) Three.           6. (A) Sally's.
   (B) Thirteen.           (B) Bob's.
   (C) Thirty.            (C) Joan's.

**8** Your turn

Complete the chart with your answers and then ask three
people about their birthdays.

| | When is your birthday? | How do you celebrate it? |
|---|---|---|
| You | | |
| Person 1 | | |
| Person 2 | | |
| Person 3 | | |

# 4 How Are You Feeling?

## 1 What's going on?

**Look at the picture and match the health problem with the person.**

1. ___ toothache

2. ___ headache

3. ___ broken leg

4. ___ broken arm

5. ___ cough

6. ___ sunburn

## 2 What's the cure?

**Listen and match the health problem with the cure. See the example.**

Health problems

1. a headache
2. a cough
3. a sunburn
4. a broken leg
5. a cut on an arm
6. a toothache

Cures

a. put on a bandage
b. wear a cast
c. take aspirin
d. put on cream
e. take cough syrup
f. take aspirin

## 3 Train your ear

**Words can have one or more syllables. Listen to the examples:**

*help* (one syllable)
*bro-ken* (two syllables)
*pharm-a-cist* (three syllables)

**Listen and circle how many syllables you hear.**

a. 1 2 3          f. 1 2 3
b. 1 2 3          g. 1 2 3
c. 1 2 3          h. 1 2 3
d. 1 2 3          i. 1 2 3
e. 1 2 3

## 4 What's the matter?

**Listen and number each pair of people.**

a.                                        c.

b.                                        d.

## 5 The best remedy

**Listen and number the pictures. Then listen again and match the picture with the correct remedies.**

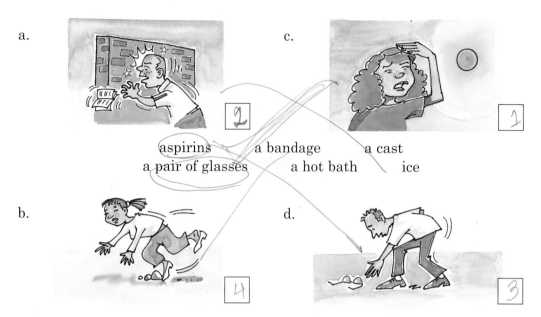

a. _2_

c. _1_

aspirins   a bandage   a cast

a pair of glasses   a hot bath   ice

b. _4_

d. _3_

## 6 Can you see this?

**Listen to people doing eye-tests and cross out the letters they miss. Then listen again and write the letters the patient saw.**

|  | Patient 1 Right Eye | Patient 1 Left Eye | Patient 2 Right Eye | Patient 3 Left Eye |
|---|---|---|---|---|
| 1. | E | E | E | E |
| 2. | HN | HN | HN | HN |
| 3. | DFN | DFN | DFN | DFN |
| 4. | PTXZ | PTXZ | PTXZ | PTXZ |
| 5. | UZDTF | UZDTF | UZDTF | UZDTF |
| 6. | DFNPTH | DFNPTH | DFNPTH | DFNPTH |
| 7. | PHUNTDZ | PHUNTDZ | PHUNTDZ | PHUNTDZ |
| 8. | NPXTZFH | NPXTZFH | NPXTZFH | NPXTZFH |

**Listen and circle the answer that matches the picture.**

1.  (A) (B) (C)

2.  (A) (B) (C)

**Listen and circle the best response.**

3. (A) (B) (C)

4. (A) (B) (C)

**Listen to the conversation and to the question that follows. Choose the best answer.**

5. (A) She put on a cast.
   (B) She fell off her bicycle.
   (C) She broke her arm.

6. (A) Some aspirin.
   (B) Playing soccer.
   (C) His ankle.

**8** Your turn

With your partner, take turns being "doctor" / "patient". Write each of the problems on a piece of paper, and turn them upside down. Pick one, and tell the "doctor" about your problem and listen to the remedies suggested. Use: *What's the problem? When did it start? You should take ..., You must ..., You have to ...*

Toothache

Headache

Broken leg

Broken arm

Cough

Sunburn

23

# Review 1

**1** Tell me about your friend

Listen to people describe their friends. Circle when they were born and their nationality. Then listen again and check (✓) the characteristics you hear.

| | | Born | Sign | Characteristics |
|---|---|---|---|---|
| 1. | Tina | 1973 / 1985<br>Moroccan / Mexican | Ox | ☐ positive<br>☑ generous<br>☑ works hard |
| 2. | Wong | 1974 / 1986<br>Japanese / Chinese | Tiger | ☑ generous<br>☑ lucky<br>☐ positive |
| 3. | Craig | 1975 / 1987<br>Colombian / Spanish | Rabbit | ☐ creative<br>☐ quiet<br>☐ friendly |
| 4. | Katie | 1976 / 1988<br>English / Spanish | Dragon | ☑ wants to be successful<br>☐ lucky<br>☑ creative |
| 5. | Paul | 1977 / 1989<br>Moroccan / French | Snake | ☑ intelligent<br>☐ selfish<br>☑ loves to talk |
| 6. | Hana | 1978 / 1990<br>Chilean / Peruvian | Horse | ☐ romantic<br>☑ intelligent<br>☑ wants to be successful |

**Listen and circle the answer that matches the picture.**

1. (A) (B) (C)

3. (A) (B) (C)

2. (A) (B) (C)

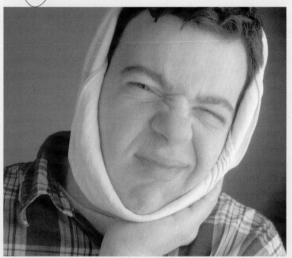

4. (A) (B) (C)

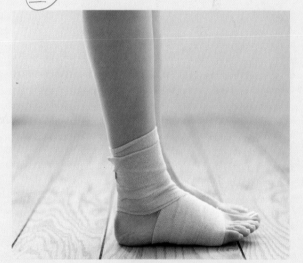

**Listen and circle the best response.**

5. (A) (B) (C)
6. (A) (B) (C)

7. (A) (B) (C)
8. (A) (B) (C)

**Listen to the conversation and to the question that follows. Circle the best answer.**

9. (A) He can't cough.
   (B) He can't stop coughing.
   (C) He feels cold.

10. (A) She's English.
    (B) She's French.
    (C) She's Canadian.

# 5 At the Mall

## 1 What's going on?

**Write the words under the store in which you would find these products and add some more of your own.**

pants    magazine    novel    cell phone
hamburger    greeting card    jacket    dictionary
phone batteries    cookbook    noodles    joystick    video game

| Video Game Store | Bookstore | Food Court | Wireless Store | Clothing Store |
|---|---|---|---|---|
| | | | | |
| | | | | |
| | | | | |
| | | | | |
| | | | | |
| | | | | |
| | | | | |
| | | | | |

## 2 What do you see?

**Listen to the statements about the picture above. Circle the correct answer.**

1. yes / no        3. yes / no        5. yes / no
2. yes / no        4. yes / no        6. yes / no

## 3 Where will they go?

**Listen and number the pictures.**

a.

3

c.

2

b.

4

d.

1

## 4 Where did we park the car?

**Listen and number the car the people are looking for.**

Train your ear

The *-ed* at the end of the past tense is pronounced in three ways. Listen to the examples:

/t/ stopp**ed**     /d/ stay**ed**     /ɪd/ repeat**ed**

Listen to the word pronounced at the end of each conversation and check (✓) the sound that you hear.

|        | 1. | 2. | 3. | 4. | 5. | 6. |
|--------|----|----|----|----|----|----|
| /t/    |    |    |    |    |    |    |
| /d/    |    |    |    |    |    |    |
| /ɪd/   |    |    |    |    |    |    |

6 Come shopping with me

Listen to Tom and Louise and number the stores in the order that they visited them.

| Shoe Store | Bookstore | Coffee Shop | Toy Store | Clothing Store | Restaurant |
|---|---|---|---|---|---|

| Computer Store | Gift Store | TV Store | Music Store | Bank | Jewelry Store |
|---|---|---|---|---|---|

Then listen again and check (✓) the things that they bought.

|               | Tom | Louise |
|---------------|-----|--------|
| boots         | ✓   | ✓      |
| socks         | ✓   | ✓      |
| jazz CDs      | ✗   | ✓      |
| classical CDs | ✓   | ✗      |
| magazine      | ✗   | ✗      |
| book          | ✓   | ✗      |
| sweater       | ✗   | ✓      |
| watch         | ✓   |        |
| picture frame |     | ✓      |
| donuts        |     |        |

**Listen and circle the answer that matches the picture.**

1. (A) _(B)_ (C)           2. (A) (B) _(C)_

**Listen and circle the best response.**

3. (A) _(B)_ (C)           4. (A) (B) (C)

**Listen to the conversation and to the question that follows. Circle the best answer.**

5. _(A)_ Her watch stopped.        6. (A) In four minutes.
   (B) She doesn't have time.       (B) In twenty minutes.
   (C) She's late for a meeting.      _(C)_ In thirty minutes.

**8**   Your turn

**What are the names of some of the stores in your mall? Which ones are your favorites? Compare your list with that of other people.**

|     | Type of store     | Names of stores |     |
| --- | ----------------- | --------------- | --- |
| 1.  | Department Stores | _____         | _____ |
| 2.  | Clothing Stores   | _____         | _____ |
| 3.  | Book Stores       | _____         | _____ |
| 4.  | _____           | _____         | _____ |
| 5.  | _____           | _____         | _____ |
| 6.  | _____           | _____         | _____ |

# 6 At the Movies

## 1 What's going on?

**Put the letters from the pictures next to the correct words.**

1. ___ director
2. ___ popcorn
3. ___ subtitles
4. ___ soundtrack

5. ___ special effect
6. ___ computer animation
7. ___ actor
8. ___ computer animators

## 2 What are they talking about?

**Listen and number each topic.**

a. ☐ animated movies
b. ☐ Chinese movies
c. ☐ special effects

d. ☐ soundtrack
e. ☐ western movies
f. ☐ popcorn

## 3 What movie did they see?

**Listen and number the posters.**

a.

b.

c.

d.

## 4 What did you like about the movie?

**Listen and check (✓) what was liked in each movie. Then listen again and check (✓) if the speakers would recommend the movie.**

1. ☐ acting  ☑ story  ☐ music  ☐ special effects  ☐ humor
   ☐ recommended

2. ☐ acting  ☐ story  ☑ music  ☐ special effects  ☑ humor
   ☐ recommended

3. ☐ acting  ☐ story  ☐ music  ☑ special effects  ☐ humor
   ☐ recommended

4. ☐ acting  ☐ story  ☐ music  ☐ special effects  ☐ humor
   ☐ recommended

## 5 Train your ear

**Words are stressed in a sentence to make sure people understand important information. Listen to the examples:**

*I think the next show starts at six p.m.*

*No, what time is the first show?*

**Listen and draw (•) over the word that is stressed.**

1. What time is the first show?
2. How much does a ticket cost?
3. It costs ten dollars.
4. I like action movies.
5. You liked Skywalkers on Mars?
6. The special effects were fantastic.
7. I'm going to buy the CD.

## 6 What time is the movie?

**Listen and cross off the times that are incorrect. Then listen again and write the correct times.**

| 1. | 2. | 3. | 4. |
|----|----|----|----|
| 12:00 ✗ | 1:45 ✓ | 11:45 ✗ | 10:00 ✗ |
| 2:47 ✓ | 4:35 ✗ | 1:10 ✓ | 12:00 ✓ |
| 5:36 ✗ | 7:50 ✓ | 3:25 ✗ | 2:38 ✓ |
| 8:00 ✓ | 10:10 ✗ | 5:50 ✗ ✓ | 4:35 ✗ |
| 10:03 ✗ | 11:30 ✗ | 7:40 ✓ | |

Test yourself

**Listen and circle the answer that matches the picture.**

1. (A) (B) (C)        2. (A) (B) (C)

**Listen and circle the best response.**

3. (A) (B) (C)        4. (A) (B) (C)

**Listen to the conversation and to the question that follows.
Circle the best answer.**

5. (A) 5:00.              6. (A) The story.
   (B) 6:00.                 (B) The special effects.
   (C) 8:30.                 (C) The music.

Your turn

**Answer the questions below and then ask your partner.
Write two questions of your own.**

|     |                                              | You | Your partner |
| --- | -------------------------------------------- | --- | ------------ |
| 1.  | How often do you go to the movies?           |     |              |
| 2.  | What kind of movies do you like best?        |     |              |
| 3.  | Who is your favorite actor or actress?       |     |              |
| 4.  | What was the last movie you saw?             |     |              |
| 5.  | What was the best movie you saw this year?   |     |              |
| 6.  |                                           ?  |     |              |
| 7.  |                                           ?  |     |              |

# 7 Dining Out

## 1 What's going on?

**Match the word with the picture.**

1. ___ today's specials
2. ___ menu
3. ___ waiter
4. ___ customer
5. ___ grilled
6. ___ fried
7. ___ baked
8. ___ chef
9. ___ steamed

## 2 What are the specials today?

**Listen and circle two of the items that are Today's Specials.**

1. Appetizer
Tomato salad
Broccoli soup ✓
Shrimp cocktail

2. Entrée
Chicken with French fries
Chicken with mashed potatoes ✓
Steamed carrots, broccoli and peas ✓

3. Side dish
Steamed spinach ✓
Rice
Baked potato ✓

4. Dessert
Chocolate cake
Lemon pie ✓
Vanilla ice cream ✓

## 3 What do you want to eat?

**Listen to the order and write the correct table number in the box.**

Entrées   *Grilled*

Chicken [1][ ][ ][ ]   Steak [2][ ][ ][ ]   Fish [ ][ ][ ][ ]   Pork chops [ ][ ][ ][ ]
Tempura [ ][ ][ ][ ]   Curry rice [3][ ][ ][ ]   Spaghetti [ ][ ][ ][ ]

Side Dishes

Rice [ ][ ][ ][ ]   Baked potato [ ][ ][ ][ ]   French fries [2][ ][ ][ ]   Salad [1][3][4][ ]
Vegetables [4][ ][ ][ ]   Apple sauce [ ][ ][ ][ ]   Miso soup [ ][ ][ ][ ]   Tofu [ ][ ][ ][ ]

Drinks

Soda [1][ ][ ][ ]   Coffee [2][ ][ ][ ]   Juice [4][ ][ ][ ]   Tea [ ][ ][ ][ ]   Water [3][ ][ ][ ]

Desserts

Cake [1][ ][ ][ ]   Ice cream [2][3][ ][ ]   Pie [ ][ ][ ][ ]

## 4 Train your ear

**There are different ways to express amounts of money and percentage figures. See the examples.**

$13.75   *thirteen dollars and seventy-five cents*
         *thirteen seventy-five*

$107.32  *one hundred and seven dollars and thirty-two cents*
         *one-oh-seven thirty-two*

8.5%     *eight and a half percent*
         *eight point five percent*

**Listen and write the amounts you hear.**

| Table 1. | Table 2. | Table 3. | Table 4. |
|---|---|---|---|
| Food total | Food total | Food total | Food total |
| $84.35 | $56.35 | $12.75 | $206 |
| Tax | Tax | Tax | Tax |
| $6.75 | $1.97 | $0.50 | $6% |
| Tip | Tip | Tip | Tip |
| $12.65 | $6.57 | $0.00 | 17% |
| Total | Total | Total | Total |
| $103.75 | $62.02 | $13.25 | |

## 5 Radio ads

**Listen and match the restaurant with the type of food served there. Then listen again and write when the restaurant opens.**

1. b.
Captain Hiro's. Opens (lunch & dinner) 11am – 12 am

2. a.
Burt's Diner. Opens (lunch & dinner) 11:30 am – 10pm

3. d.
Iceland. Opens 11:30am – 9pm

4. c
Sam's All Night Café. Opens 8pm – 8am

a.        b.        c.        d.

## 6 Where's the café?

**Listen and number the phrases. Then listen again and put the phrases in the right spaces.**

a. [3] across the street from
b. [ ] between
c. [ ] next to
d. [ ] on the corner of

e. the café across the street from the diner
f. the café _____ next to _____ the bank
g. the café _____ on the corner of _____ Main and Elm streets
h. the café _____ between, _____ the diner and bank

36

Test yourself

**Listen and circle the answer that matches the picture.**

1. (A)  (B)  (C)           2. (A)  (B)  (C)

**Listen and circle the best response.**

3. (A)  (B)  (C)           4. (A)  (B)  (C)

**Listen to the conversation and to the question that follows.
Circle the best answer.**

5. (A) at 12:30.           6. (A) Hamburgers.
   (B) at 1:00.               (B) Italian food.
   (C) at 1:30.  Joe's        (C) Seafood.
       cafe

**8** Your turn

**With two other people, take turns talking about your favorite
restaurant. Complete the chart.**

|  | You | Person 1 | Person 2 |
|---|---|---|---|
| What is your favorite restaurant? |  |  |  |
| Where is it located? |  |  |  |
| What kind of food do they serve? |  |  |  |
| Why do you like it so much? |  |  |  |

# 8 What Are You Wearing?

a.          b.          c.          d.          e.

## 1 What's going on?

**Look at the picture and match the clothes with the person.**

1. ___ backward baseball cap
2. ___ three earrings in one ear
3. ___ do-rag
4. ___ gold necklace
5. ___ long-sleeved shirt
6. ___ sunglasses
7. ___ striped blouse
8. ___ nose ring

9. ___ ripped jeans
10. ___ tattoo
11. ___ button-down shirt
12. ___ T-shirt
13. ___ black leather boots
14. ___ red sneakers
15. ___ high heels

## 2 What are you wearing?

**Listen and circle the clothing that you hear.**

1. short-sleeved shirt / long-sleeved shirt ✓
2. black shoes ✓ / brown shoes
3. red skirt / red shirt ✓
4. low heels / high heels ✓
5. blue jeans ✓ / blue pants
6. ripped T-shirt ✓ / striped shirt

**3** What day's it on?

The *-s* at the end of plural words is pronounced in three ways. Listen to the examples:

boots /s/    rings /z/    purses /ɪz/

**Listen to the words and check (✓) the sound you hear.**

|  | /s/ | /z/ | /ɪz/ |
|---|---|---|---|
| watches | ✓ |  |  |
| jackets |  | (z) |  |
| jeans |  |  | (ɪz) |

|  | /s/ | /z/ | /ɪz/ |
|---|---|---|---|
| earrings | ✓ |  |  |
| necklaces | /s/ |  |  |
| shirts | /s/ |  |  |

**4** On or off?

**Listen and circle the correct clothes. Then listen again. Do the people *put on or take off* the clothes? Circle the correct verb.**

1. (A) blue shoes
   (B) black shoes
   put on / take off

2. (A) jacket
   (B) jeans
   put on / take off

3. (A) striped sweater
   (B) plain-colored sweater
   put on / take off

## 5  What should I wear?

**Listen and number the correct three people in the picture.**

| a | | b | | c | | d | | e | | f | |
|---|---|---|---|---|---|---|---|---|---|---|---|

## 6  The right clothes

**Listen and match the occasion with the person.**

1. ☑ School dance (b)
2. ☑ Picnic (c)
3. ☐ Job interview (a)
4. ☐ Formal dance (d)

a.

b.

c.

d.

**Listen and circle the answer that matches the picture.**

1. (A) (B) (C)            2. (A) (B) (C)

**Listen and circle the best response.**

3. (A) (B) (C)            4. (A) (B) (C)

**Listen to the conversation and to the question that follows. Circle the best answer.**

5. (A) Striped.            6. (A) A new dress.
  (B) Inexpensive.              (B) A black dress.
  (C) Green.              (C) A long dress.

**8** Your turn

**Sit back to back with your partner. Choose one of the people in the unit and describe them. Can your partner find the person you are describing quickly? Now change roles.**

**Start by saying *X is wearing* ...**

| | | |
|---|---|---|
| short / long-sleeved shirt | sunglasses | blouse |
| jeans | boots | T-shirt |
| high heels | jacket | ring |
| a pair of earrings | | |

# Review 2

**1** Where do you want to eat?

Listen and put the restaurant names in the right places on the map. Choose from the list: *Pyramids, Mabel's Café, River House Restaurant, Windsor Diner, Café Rossi.*

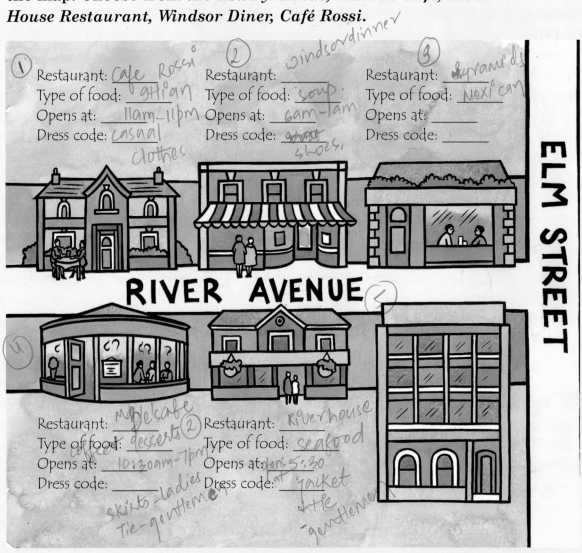

① Restaurant: _Cafe Rossi_
Type of food: _Italian_
Opens at: _11am-11pm_
Dress code: _casual clothes_

② Restaurant: _windsordinner_
Type of food: _soup_
Opens at: _6am-7am_
Dress code: _shorts shoes_

③ Restaurant: _pyramids_
Type of food: _Mexican_
Opens at: _____
Dress code: _____

**RIVER AVENUE**

④ Restaurant: _mabelscafe_
Type of food: _coffee desserts_
Opens at: _10:30am-7pm_
Dress code: _skirts-ladies Tie-gentlemen_

⑤ Restaurant: _Riverhouse_
Type of food: _seafood_
Opens at: _opens 5:30_
Dress code: _jacket tie gentlemen_

**ELM STREET**

Then listen again. Write the time the restaurant opens and the type of food it serves. Choose the food from: *Italian, desserts and coffee, seafood, soup, Mexican.*

Can you remember the dress code for each restaurant? Choose from the list: *skirt and a tie, business suit, shorts and T-shirt, casual pants and T-shirt.*

## 2 Conversation review

**Listen and circle the answer that matches the pictures.**

1. (A)  (B)  (C)

3. (A)  (B)  (C)

2. (A)  (B)  (C)

4. (A)  (B)  (C)

**Listen and circle the best response.**

5. (A)  (B)  (C)

6. (A)  (B)  (C)

7. (A)  (B)  (C)

8. (A)  (B)  (C)

**Listen to the conversation and to the question that follows. Circle the best answer.**

9. (A) 5:00.

   (B) 5:30.

   (C) 6:30.

10. (A) A dress and shoes.

    (B) A dress and a jacket.

    (C) A dress, a jacket and shoes.

# 9 Traffic Jam

## 1 What's going on?

**Look at the picture and match the two parts of each sentence.**

1. The drivers are honking ...
2. A police officer is directing ...
3. A man is fixing ...
4. The passengers are riding ...
5. Someone is flying ...
6. A man is riding ...

a. a helicopter.
b. a bicycle.
c. a flat tire.
d. traffic.
e. their horns.
f. the bus.

## 2 How are you getting there?

**Listen and match each person with the way she/he travels.**

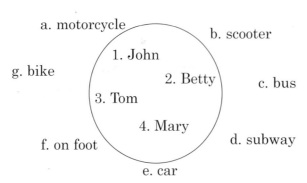

a. motorcycle
b. scooter
g. bike
c. bus
f. on foot
d. subway
e. car

1. John
2. Betty
3. Tom
4. Mary

## 3 Don't talk to me like that!

**Listen and number the pictures.**

a.

c.

b.

d.

## 4 Train your ear

Sometimes, the only difference between two words is one sound. Listen to the examples:

*My **feet** hurt.* /iː/      *These sandals don't **fit**.* /ɪ/

Listen to the conversations and pay attention to the word repeated at the end. Check (✓) the column of the sound you hear.

|      | 1. | 2. | 3. | 4. |
|------|----|----|----|----|
| /iː/ | ✓  | ✓  |    |    |
| /ɪ/  |    |    | ✓  | ✓  |

45

### 5 A better way to go

**Listen and write *W* (woman) and *M* (man).**

1.

|  | On foot | By car |
|---|---|---|
| more comfortable |  | W |
| healthier | M |  |
| faster |  | W |
| drier |  | W |

3.

|  | By motorcycle | By car |
|---|---|---|
| more comfortable |  | M |
| more expensive |  | W |
| more fun | W |  |
| faster | W |  |
| colder |  | M |

2.

|  | By bus | By car |
|---|---|---|
| more comfortable |  | W |
| more convenient |  | M |
| slower | M |  |
| cleaner | M |  |

4.

|  | By bicycle | On the subway |
|---|---|---|
| more comfortable | W |  |
| more convenient | M |  |
| more expensive |  | M |
| faster |  | M |

### 6 What's the problem?

**Listen and number the picture.**

a.

c.

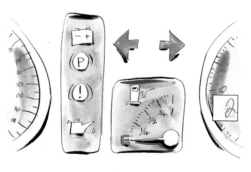

b.

d.

46

**Listen and circle the answer that matches the picture.**

1. (A)  (B)  (C)

2. (A)  (B)  (C)

**Listen and circle the best response.**

3. (A)  (B)  (C)

4. (A)  (B)  (C)

**Listen to the conversation and to the question that follows.
Circle the best answer.**

5. (A) By subway.
(B) By bus.
(C) By car.

6. (A) A car.
(B) A bicycle.
(C) A bus.

**8** Your turn

**Complete the survey for you and three people. Use:** *How do
you get to school? Why do you use this form of transportation?*

|  | Transport | Why do you use it? |
|---|---|---|
| You |  |  |
| Person 1 |  |  |
| Person 2 |  |  |
| Person 3 |  |  |

# 10 On the Weekend

## 1 What's going on?

**Match the activity with the picture.**

1. ___ have coffee with friends
2. ___ reading
3. ___ run errands
4. ___ go out of town
5. ___ go for a bike ride
6. ___ clean the house
7. ___ go to the movies
8. ___ play computer games

## 2 What do you want to do?

**Listen and number the activities.**

a. [4] go to a movie
b. [1] have a coffee
c. [5] take a bike ride
d. [6] play video games
e. [3] clean up
f. [2] go to the bookstore

## 3 Where and when?

**Listen and write the order of each activity.**

1. [4] meet at the café   [3] ride bikes   [4] go to the movies
2. [3] read a book   [2] go to the movies   [1] go shopping
3. [4] clean the house   [2] drive to the beach   [3] return the library books
4. [1] go to the grocery   [3] go to the bakery   [2] go to the library
   [1] store

## 4 Things to do today

**Listen and check (✔) what George and Lisa did.**

**George**

1. ☑ bought steaks
   ☑ bought coffee and sugar
   ☐ bought cookies
   ☐ bought soda
   ☑ returned library books

2. ☐ bought cat food
   ☑ bought toy for cat

3. ☑ mailed letters
   ☑ bought stamps
   ☐ rode my bike

4. ☑ bought bread
   ☑ bought cookies
   ☐ bought paint
   ☐ left town

**Lisa**

1. ☐ painted the bathroom
   ☑ cleaned the kitchen

2. ☐ painted the bathroom
   ☐ talked to my sister
   ☑ went for coffee with
      my sister

3. ☐ went to the movies
   ☑ watched TV

4. ☑ made a tuna sandwich
   ☐ painted the bathroom

## 5 Train your ear

The contractions *he's* and *she's* can sound similar.
Listen to the examples:

*He's* talking on a cell phone.   *She's* talking on a cell phone.

**Listen and check (✓) in the right column the contraction you hear.**

|       | 1. | 2. | 3. | 4. | 5. | 6. |
|-------|----|----|----|----|----|----|
| She's |    |    | ✓  | ✓  | ✓  |    |
| He's  | ✓  | ✓  |    |    |    | ✓  |

## 6 It was a great weekend

**Listen and number the pictures. Then listen again and match the picture with the word that best describes the weekend.**

a.

Exciting

Boring

c.

b.

Relaxing

d.

Busy

50

**Listen and circle the answer that matches the picture.**

1. (A) (B) (C)

2. (A) (B) (C)

**Listen and circle the best response.**

3. (A) (B) (C)

4. (A) (B) (C)

**Listen to the conversation and to the question that follows. Circle the best answer.**

5. (A) He cleaned the house.
   (B) He went to the movies.
   (C) He played tennis.

6. (A) To a bakery.
   (B) To a paint store.
   (C) To a café.

**8** Your turn

**Answer these questions about your weekend and then ask two people the same questions.**

|  | You | Person 1 | Person 2 |
|---|---|---|---|
| What did you do this weekend? |  |  |  |
| What are you going to do next weekend? |  |  |  |

# 11 Room Service

## 1 What's going on?

**Put the letters from the picture next to the correct words.**

1. ___ bedroom
2. ___ pool
3. ___ fitness center
4. ___ lobby

5. ___ tennis court
6. ___ restaurant
7. ___ swimming
8. ___ checking in

9. ___ playing tennis
10. ___ eating
11. ___ room service
12. ___ doing exercises

## 2 Do you have a reservation?

**Listen and check (✓) the correct name.**

1. ☐ Takumi Hosawa
   ☑ Takumi Osawa
2. ☑ Ms. Crenshaw
   ☐ Ms. Wilson

3. ☑ Joseph Krane
   ☐ Joseph Crane
4. ☐ Ms. Toby
   ☑ Ms. Thaughby

## 3 Train your ear

**It can be difficult to hear the difference between the singular and the plural. Listen and circle the correct word and if it is plural then write the pronunciation /s/, /z/ or /ɪz/.**

1. a. ☐ pool     b. ☑ /z/ pools      4. a. ☑ television    b. ☐ televisions
    c. ☑ tennis court   d. ☐ tennis courts      c. ☐ telephone    d. ☑ telephones
2. a. ☑ room     b. ☐ rooms      5. a. ☐ peach    b. ☑ peaches
    c. ☐ bed     d. ☑ beds      c. ☑ restaurant    d. ☐ restaurants
3. a. ☑ glass of milk    b. ☐ glasses of milk
    c. ☐ cup of coffee    d. ☑ cups of coffee

## 4 Checking in

**Listen and check (✓) the correct pictures. Then listen again and write the number of nights they will stay.**

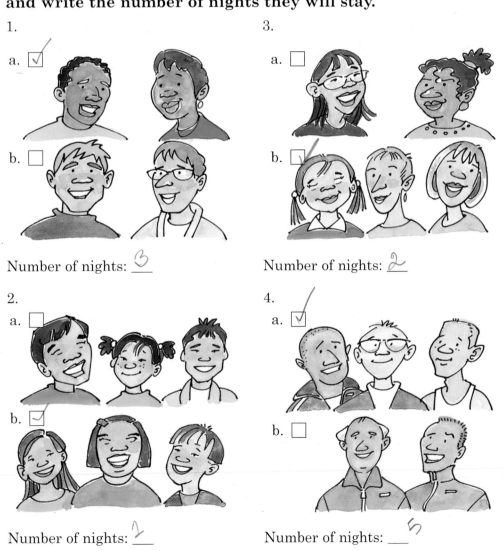

1.
a. ☑
b. ☐
Number of nights: _3_

3.
a. ☐
b. ☑
Number of nights: _2_

2.
a. ☐
b. ☑
Number of nights: _1_

4.
a. ☑
b. ☐
Number of nights: _5_

## 5 Hotel services

**Listen and check (✓) the services that each hotel offers.
Then listen again and correct the times and numbers that
are wrong.**

| Grand Hotel | Beach Hotel | Barbara's Bed and Breakfast |
|---|---|---|
| ☐ Airport transfers | ☐ Airport transfers | ☐ Airport transfers |
| ☐ Bar | ☐ Bar | ☐ Bar |
| ✓ Business center | ☐ Business center | ☐ Business center |
| ☐ Beach | ✓ Beach | ☐ Beach |
| ☐ Coffee shop | ☐ Coffee shop | ☐ Coffee shop |
| ✓ Fitness center | ✓ Fitness center | ☐ Fitness center |
| ✓ Shopping arcade | ☐ Shopping arcade | ☐ Shopping arcade |
| ☐ Golf course | ✓ Golf course | ☐ Golf course |
| ✓ Internet access | ☐ Internet access | ☐ Internet access |
| ✓ Meeting rooms | ☐ Meeting rooms | ☐ Meeting rooms |
| ☐ Pool | ✓ Pool | ☐ Pool |
| ☐ Restaurant | ✓ Restaurant | ☐ Restaurant |
| ☐ Room service | ✓ Room service | ☐ Room service |
| ☐ Spa | ☐ Spa | ☐ Spa |
| ☐ Tennis court | ✓ Tennis court | ☐ Tennis court |
| Check-in time: 3 p.m.<br>Check-out time: noon | Check-in time: 4 p.m.<br>Check-out time: noon | Check-in time: noon<br>Check-out time: 10 a.m. 9am |
| Number of rooms: ~~150~~ 115 | Number of rooms: 219 | Number of rooms: ~~40~~ 4 |
| Toll-free number<br>1-800-5~~15~~ 55-1234 | Toll-free number<br>1-888-292-~~2929~~ 92 | Toll-free number<br>1-877-345-3434 |

## 6 Hotel reservations

**Listen and complete the chart.**

|  | a. | b. | c. | d. |
|---|---|---|---|---|
| Number of rooms | 1 | 1 | 2 | 7 |
| Number of beds | 3 | 2 | 1 | 8 |
| Number of nights | 2 | 3 | 1 | 4 |

**Listen and circle the answer that matches the picture.**

1. (A) (B) (C)

2. (A) (B) (C)

**Listen and circle the best response.**

3. (A) (B) (C)

4. (A) (B) (C)

**Listen to the conversation and to the question that follows. Circle the best answer.**

5. (A) Two people.
   (B) Three people.
   (C) Four people.

6. (A) The pool.
   (B) The beach.
   (C) The fitness center.

**8** Your turn

With your partner, take turns playing a hotel receptionist and a customer. As the "customer" use: *What facilities does your hotel have? What are the check-in and check-out times?* As the "receptionist" write the name and the facilities of the hotel and complete the reservation form. Use: *Can I have your name? What's your address and telephone number? How many rooms will you require? How many nights are you going to stay?*

Hotel: _____
Facilities:

_____

_____

_____

Check-in time: _____
Check-out time: _____

**Reservation form**
Name: _____
Address: _____

Telephone number: _____

How many rooms?:_____
How many beds?: _____
How many nights?:_____

# 12 Getting Away

a

b

## 1 What's going on?

**Match the word or phrase with the picture or pictures. See the example.**

1. _a_ tour bus
2. ___ tour guide
3. ___ group tour
4. ___ solo tourist
5. ___ taking photos
6. ___ guidebooks
7. ___ art
8. ___ museum
9. ___ jet skiing
10. ___ scuba diving
11. ___ windsurfing
12. ___ snorkeling
13. _a/b_ umbrella

## 2 What do you want to do?

**Listen and number the activities.**

a. 3 go windsurfing
b. 2 visit a museum
c. 1 go on own tour
d. 4 go scuba diving
e. 5 go on a guided tour

## 3 Train your ear

**When *is* is contracted to *'s*, it is pronounced in the same way as plural *-s*. Listen to the example:**

*The statue's / statues open from 9:30 to 5:00 every day.*

**Listen and circle the correct word.**

1. city's / cities
2. visitor's / visitors
3. continent's / continents
4. hand's / hands
5. nose's / noses

6. finger's / fingers
7. arm's / arms
8. lip's / lips
9. step's / steps

## 4 Planning the getaway

**Listen and cross out the picture that did not happen.**

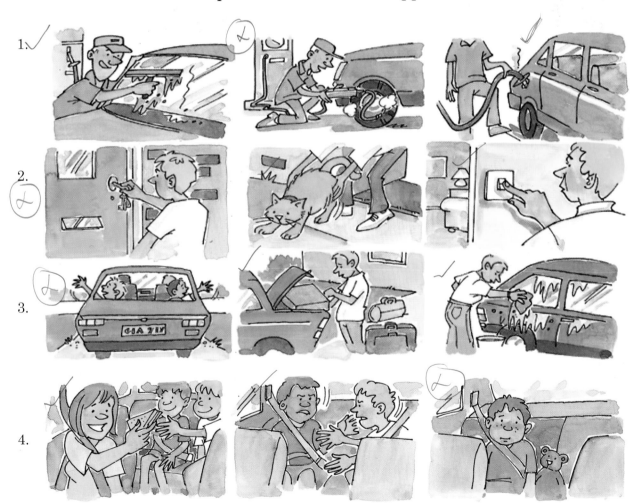

1.
2.
3.
4.

57

## 5 Picture this

**Listen and number the pictures.**

a.

c.

b.
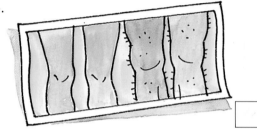

d.

## 6 Sightseeing

**Listen and number the tourists' notes. Then listen again and circle the correct information.**

a.

Los Angeles Memorial Stadium
Built: 1923 / 1932
Last Olympics: 1932 / 1984
Number of seats: 16,000 / 68,000
Web site:   www.citylastad.net /
www.la_stadium.org

c.

Hollwood / Hollywood Sign
Built   1975 / 1923
Tall:   4.5 meters / 45 meters
Length: 137 meters / 127 meters
Web site:   www.hollywoodsign.net /
www.holleywd.com

b.

LA Museum of Contemporary Art
Built: 1918 / 1982
Architect: Japanese / Javanese
Warhol exhibit dates: May 15 to Aug 8
/ May 25 to Aug 18
Membership fee: $16 / $60
Web site:   www.cityla-art.com /
www.lacity-art.com.

d.

Hollywood and Vine
Famous: center of sports, movie
studios, radio stations, TV
Started: 1958 / 1915
Walk of Fame: 2000 / 200 stars
Web:   www.hollywoodchamber.com /
www.hollywoodchamber.us

Test yourself

**Listen and circle the answer that matches the picture.**

1. (A) (B) (C)

2. (A) (B) (C)

**Listen and circle the best response.**

3. (A) (B) (C)

4. (A) (B) (C)

**Listen to the conversation and to the question that follows. Circle the best answer.**

5. (A) Go out to eat.
   (B) Hike in the country.
   (C) Watch sports on TV.

6. (A) Go to the museum.
   (B) Windsurf.
   (C) Swim in the lake.

**8** Your turn

**Answer these questions. Then ask your partner about a recent trip. Add two questions of your own.**

|  | You | Your partner |
|---|---|---|
| 1. Where did you go? |  |  |
| 2. Who did you go with? |  |  |
| 3. How long did you stay? |  |  |
| 4. What did you see? |  |  |
| 5. |  |  |
| 6. |  |  |

# Review 3

**1** **Where? Who?**

Listen and number six places. Then listen again and match the place with the person. See the example.

a. ☑ parking garage     e. ☑ café
b. ☑ hotel     f. ☑ bus
c. ☐ library     g. ☑ shoe store
d. ☐ hospital     h. ☐ tennis court

1.

_____bus_____

3.

_shoe store_

5.

_Parking garage._

2.

_hotel_

4.

_cafe_

6.

_Library_

60

**Listen and circle the answer that matches the picture.**

1. (A) (B) (C)

3. (A) (B) (C)

2. (A) (B) (C)

4. (A) (B) (C)

**Listen and circle the best reponse.**

5. (A) (B) (C)

6. (A) (B) (C)

7. (A) (B) (C)

8. (A) (B) (C)

**Listen to the conversation and to the question that follows.
Circle the best answer.**

9. (A) See a movie.

(B) Go windsurfing.

(C) Take a bus tour.

10. (A) In a hotel.

(B) At home.

(C) In a restaurant.

# 13 The Ceiling is Leaking!

## 1 What's going on?

**Look at the picture and write the floor where there's a problem.**

1. _third floor_ leaking ceiling
2. _____ no heat
3. _____ too noisy
4. _____ needs painting

5. _____ broken window
6. _____ leaking refrigerator
7. _____ broken light
8. _____ bugs

## 2 What do you see?

**Listen to the statements about the picture above. Circle the correct answer.**

1. yes / no
2. yes / no
3. yes / no

4. yes / no
5. yes / no
6. yes / no

Cardinal numbers (e.g. *one*, *two*) sound different from ordinal numbers (e.g. *first*, *second*). Listen to the examples:

*I live in Apartment **9A**.*
*I live on the **ninth** floor.*

**Listen and write the numbers.**

| | Floor | Apartment no. |
|---|---|---|
| 1. | First floor. | 1A |
| 2. | Second floor | 2D. |
| 3. | 4th floor | 4F |
| 4. | Seventh floor | 7H |

**Listen and check (✓) the correct problem.**

|  | A | | B |
|---|---|---|---|
| 1. | ☑ | | ☐ The apartment's too hot. |
| 2. | ☑ | | ☐ The apartment is too small. |
| 3. | ☑ | | ☑ There's water coming through the ceiling. |
| 4. | ☑ | | ☐ The phone doesn't work. |

## 5 Where is everyone?

**Listen and cross off the names that are not correct. Then listen again and correct them.**

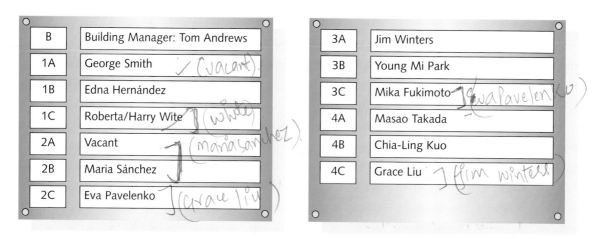

| | |
|---|---|
| B | Building Manager: Tom Andrews |
| 1A | George Smith ✓ (vacant) |
| 1B | Edna Hernández |
| 1C | Roberta/Harry Wite ✓ (white) (maria sanchez) |
| 2A | Vacant |
| 2B | Maria Sánchez |
| 2C | Eva Pavelenko (Grace Liu) |

| | |
|---|---|
| 3A | Jim Winters |
| 3B | Young Mi Park |
| 3C | Mika Fukimoto (Eva Pavelenko) |
| 4A | Masao Takada |
| 4B | Chia-Ling Kuo |
| 4C | Grace Liu (Jim winters) |

## 6 You pay how much?

**Listen and number the apartment plans. Then listen again and write the monthly rent and circle whether utilities are included or not.**

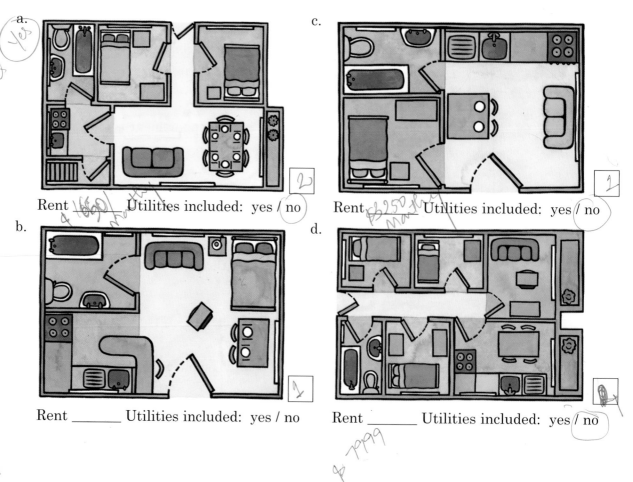

a. $4000 utilities yes

Rent $1600 monthly    Utilities included:  yes / **no**    2

c.

Rent $250 monthly    Utilities included:  yes / **no**    1

b.

Rent _____    Utilities included:  yes / no    1

d.

Rent _____    Utilities included:  yes / no    $999

## 7 Test yourself

**Listen and circle the answer that matches the picture.**

1. (A) (B) (C)

2. (A) (B) (C)

**Listen and circle the best response.**

3. (A) (B) (C)

4. (A) (B) (C)

**Listen to the conversation and to the question that follows. Circle the best answer.**

5. (A) The heat doesn't work.
   (B) The window is broken.
   (C) The manager is away.

6. (A) $200/month.
   (B) $300/month.
   (C) $400/month.

## 8 Your turn

**Draw your home floor plan. Write good and bad points about it. Now ask your partner. Use:** *Please describe your floor plan. Tell me two good and two bad points about the place where you live.*

Your floor plan

Two good things about where you live:
•
•

Bad points:
•
•

Your partner's floor plan

Two good things about where they live:
•
•

Bad points:
•
•

# 14 Stay in Touch

## 1 What's going on?

**Match the word with the picture.**

1. ___ pager
2. ___ cell phone
3. ___ monitor
4. ___ computer
5. ___ laptop
6. ___ Internet browser
7. ___ e-mail
8. ___ mouse
9. ___ keyboard
10. ___ fax machine
11. ___ photocopier

## 2 What's that noise?

**Listen to the sounds and number the items below.**

a. ___ pager
b. ___ keyboard
c. ___ cell phone
d. ___ fax machine
e. ___ modem
f. ___ photocopier
g. ___ e-mail

## 3 What does it do?

**Listen to the radio ads and circle the correct words. Then listen again and write the price.**

1.

> The Lextronic LS 565 pager.
> The best pager on the market.
>
> **Features:**
> Choose from ((5) / 15) rings.
> Holds up to ((14) / 40) messages.
> Requires ("AA / (AAA)") battery.
> Price: $_99.99_

3.

> **APEX Fax Machine**
> The X400 model is perfect for the home office
>
> *Features:*
> *((Uses) / Doesn't use) plain paper*
> *((100) / 200)-page fax capability.*
> *((256) / 512)K memory stores up*
> *to (12 / (20)) pages.*
> *Price: $_150_*

2.

> Speedy Access
>
> The premier Internet Service Provider in the metro area.
>
> Features:
> (Limited / (Unlimited)) Internet access. ((10) / 100) MB of free Web space. ((8) / 16) mailboxes.
> Price: $_29.95_ /month

4.

> **Wireless World's KX Series cell phone**
> *The hottest cell phone on the market.*
> *Free with our monthly plan.*
>
> *Features:*
> *Latest ((KX 100) / KX 1100) model*
> *(100 / (1000)) free cell phone minutes a month.*
> *((2) / 20) Voice mailboxes*
>
> Price $_39.95_ a month.

## 4 How can I reach you?

**Listen and number the pictures.**

a.

2

c.

4

b.

1

d.

3

## 5 How do you work this thing?

**Listen and number the people in the picture. Then listen again and match the solution with the problem.**

a.

c.

b.

d.

Solutions

e. [b] Open the cover. Pull out the paper.

f. [c] Turn down the volume.

g. [d] Put the plug into the outlet.

h. [a] Add paper.

## 6 Train your ear

**The words *can* and *can't* often sound similar when spoken. Listen to the examples:**

*You **can** buy it for $10.95.*     *You **can't** buy it for $9.95.*

**Listen and circle the correct word.**

1. can / can't
2. can / can't
3. can / can't
4. can / can't

5. can / can't
6. can / can't
7. can / can't
8. can / can't

**Listen and circle the answer that matches the picture.**

1. (A) (B) (C)          2. (A) (B) (C)

**Listen and circle the best response.**

3. (A) (B) (C)          4. (A) (B) (C)

**Listen to the conversation and to the question that follows. Circle the best answer.**

5. (A) 483-4545. *(1 homeNo.)*          6. (A) By e-mail.
   (B) 483-5445.                            (B) By mail.
   (C) 483-5454. *(fax No.)*                (C) By fax. *(fax machine broken)*

**8** Your turn

**How do you stay in touch? Complete the chart for two people you know. Then ask your partner and complete their chart. Use:** *Who do you stay in touch with? Do you telephone / page / fax / e-mail?*

| People you stay in touch with | | | | | |
|---|---|---|---|---|---|
| Name | by telephone | by pager | by fax | by e-mail | other |
| 1. | | | | | |
| 2. | | | | | |

| People your partner stays in touch with | | | | | |
|---|---|---|---|---|---|
| Name | by telephone | by pager | by fax | by e-mail | other |
| 1. | | | | | |
| 2. | | | | | |

# 15 Call Me on My Cell

## 1 What's going on?

**Look at the picture and match the activity with the person.**

1. _g_ walking a dog in the park
2. _c_ directing traffic at an intersection
3. _f_ sitting on a bench in the park
4. _h_ sitting in a car stuck in traffic
5. _b_ going shopping at a grocery store
6. _d_ playing video games in an arcade
7. _h_ riding in cars around town
8. _e_ playing on swings in the park

## 2 Who are you talking to?

**Listen to some of the people in the picture. Who is talking?**

1. _c_ and _a_
2. _h_ and _d_
3. _f_ and _h_
4. _g_ and _a_

70

### 3 What's your number?

Listen and check (✓) whether the number is their cell, home or work phone number. Then listen again and correct the number.

1. ✓ Cell    ___ Home    ___ Work    Number: 587-9392 *9293*
2. ✓ Cell    ___ Home    ___ Work    Number: 458-3233 *3232*
3. ___ Cell    ___ Home    ✓ Work    Number: 245-8897 *9987*
4. ✓ Cell    ___ Home    ___ Work    Number: 395-4499 *4949*

### 4 Send me a message

Listen and number the text messages. Then listen again and match the message with the person who received it.

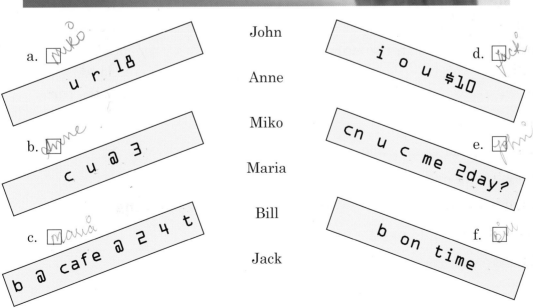

John

Anne

Miko

Maria

Bill

Jack

a. *Miko*   u r 18

b. *Anne*   c u @ 3

c. *Maria*   b @ cafe @ 2 4 t

d. *Jack*   i o u $10

e. *John*   cn u c me 2day?

f. *Bill*   b on time

71

## 5 Getting there?

**Listen and number Tina's activities. Then listen again. What's Doug doing? Match Tina's activity with the picture of Doug.**

a. ☑ Tina is walking.

b. ☑ Tina is leaving the office.

c. ☑ Tina is sitting at home.

d. ☑ Tina is sitting in traffic.

e.

f.

g.

h.

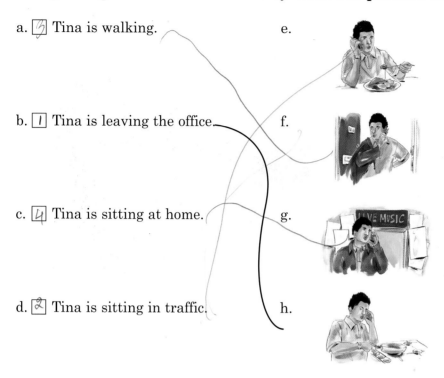

## 6 Train your ear

**You can say _yes_ and _no_ with these sounds and intonations. Listen to the examples:**

*uh huh* (yes);   *uh huh* (no);   *uh huh* (I'm listening)

**Listen and check (✓) in the correct column.**

|  | Yes | No | I'm listening |
|---|---|---|---|
| 1. Can you hear me? |  |  |  |
| 2. Stop playing that video game, now! |  |  |  |
| 3. You don't have my number, do you? |  |  |  |
| 4. Are you hungry? |  |  |  |
| 5. You're not listening to me, are you? |  |  |  |
| 6. Please take your cousin to the park. |  |  |  |

**Listen and circle the answer that matches the picture.**

1. (A) (B) (C)                    2. (A) (B) (C)

**Listen and circle the best response.**

3. (A) (B) (C)                    4. (A) (B) (C)

**Listen to the conversation and to the question that follows. Circle the best answer.**

5. (A) There's too much noise on the line.
   (B) The man is not there.
   (C) The woman is hanging up.

6. (A) At the movies.
   (B) At the travel agency.
   (C) In Tokyo.

**Do you have a cell phone? A home phone? A work phone? What's the number of each phone? Who calls you at each number? Who do you call from each phone? Complete the chart, then ask your partner the same questions.**

|  | Home phone | Cell phone | Work phone |
|---|---|---|---|
| You<br>What's the number?<br>Who calls you?<br>Who do you call? |  |  |  |
| Your partner<br>What's your number?<br>Who calls you?<br>Who do you call? |  |  |  |

# 16 Job Fair

## 1 What's going on?

**Match the word with the picture. Then cross out the word *not* related to the job.**

1. ___ pilot: train / flying / plane
2. ___ programmer: hardware / software / calculator
3. ___ architect: plans / sea / building
4. ___ journalist: poetry / reporting / newspaper
5. ___ pharmacist: grain / medicine / prescription
6. ___ dentist: toothbrush / scientist / drill
7. ___ mechanic: repair / machine / sew
8. ___ business person: office / client / radio

## 2 What do they do?

**Listen and circle the correct job. Then listen again and write the number of years people have been in their jobs.**

1. pilot / journalist _7_ years in the job
2. teacher / dentist _20_ years in the job
3. mechanic / programmer _25_ years in the job
4. architect / pharmacist _10_ years in the job

## 3 Train your ear

**You can use a tag question to ask a question or confirm a fact. Listen to the examples:**

*You're a teacher, aren't you?*
(I'm not sure. You might be a doctor. Intonation rises for question.)

*You've been a teacher for ten years, haven't you?*
(I'm sure you've been a teacher for ten years. Intonation falls for confirmation.)

**Listen and check (✓) if the speaker is sure or unsure.**

|     | Sure | Unsure |
| --- | --- | --- |
| 1.  |     |     |
| 2.  |     |     |
| 3.  |     |     |
| 4.  |     |     |

|     | Sure | Unsure |
| --- | --- | --- |
| 5.  |     |     |
| 6.  |     |     |
| 7.  |     |     |
| 8.  |     |     |

## 4 Who earns the most?

**Listen and check (✓) the person who gets paid the most. Then listen and complete the information about salary and the number of years she or he has worked.**

1. a. ✓ housekeeper          b. ☐ teacher

   Salary: _$700 a week_          Years in the job: _20 years_

2. a. ☐ computer programmer          b. ✓ lawyer

   Salary: _7000/monthly_          Years in the job: _10 years_

3. a. ☐ secretary          b. ✓ waitress

   Salary: _60000/yearly_          Years in the job: _1 year_

4. a. ☐ travel agent          b. ✓ pharmacist

   Salary: _2 years ago_          Years in the job: _70000/yearly_

## 5 Do you like your job?

**Listen and number the pictures. Then listen again and check (✓) what she/he likes best about the job.**

a.

4

What they like best:
✓ patients ___ doctors

c.

2

What they like best:
___ routine ✓ designing buildings

b.

3

What they like best:
___ helping people ✓ traveling

d.

1

What they like best:
✓ money ___ study

## 6 Choosing a job

**Listen and circle the job each person has now. Then listen again and write the job or jobs the speaker had in the past.**

| Current job | | | Past job(s) |
|---|---|---|---|
| 1. artist | waitress | architect | _waitress, artist,_ |
| 2. dentist | auto mechanic | office worker | _office worker, dentist_ |
| 3. pilot | bus driver | taxi cab driver | _taxi cab driver, bus driver_ |
| 4. journalist | pharmacist | science teacher | _science teacher,_ |

**Listen and circle the answer that matches the picture.**

1. (A) (B) (C)       2. (A) (B) (C)

**Listen and circle the best response.**

3. (A) (B) (C)       4. (A) (B) (C)

**Listen to the conversation and to the question that follows. Circle the best answer.**

5. (A) Two weeks. *ago*          6. (A) He's a writer.
   (B) Two years.                    (B) He's a student.
   (C) Twenty years.                 (C) He's a teacher.

**8** Your turn

**Complete the chart about the jobs of two people you know. Then ask your partner. Use: *What jobs do they do? What two words do you associate with each job?***

People you know

| Name | Job | Two words associated with the job |
|------|-----|-----------------------------------|
| 1. | | |
| 2. | | |

People your partner knows

| Name | Job | Two words associated with the job |
|------|-----|-----------------------------------|
| 1. | | |
| 2. | | |

# Review 4

**1** How can I help you?

**Listen and number each problem. Then listen again and write the day someone will come to fix the problem.**

a.

_____ 3 (Pest control) on Thursday

b.

_____ 2 (Lawyer)

c.

_____ 1 (Marks Plumbing)

d.

_____ 6 (monday morning)

e.

_____ 4 (day after tomorrow — on Monday)

f.

_____ 5 (on Tuesday)

**2** How can I reach you?

**Listen and circle how each speaker can be contacted. Then listen again and write the correct number.**

Speakers can be contacted by...
- cell / pager
- fax / e-mail
- cell / fax
- fax / home phone
- fax / pager
- cell / home phone

Speakers can be contacted on...

484-1770

484-1770

Mary@macmillan.com

658- — 770-771-2390

439-5443 (349-8433)

662-2613 (602-2603)

850-221990

**Listen and circle the answer that matches the picture.**

1. (A) (B) (C)

3. (A) (B) (C)

2. (A) (B) (C)

4. (A) (B) (C)

**Listen and circle the best response.**

5. (A) (B) (C)        7. (A) (B) (C)

6. (A) (B) (C)        8. (A) (B) (C)

**Listen to the conversation and to the question that follows. Circle the best answer.**

9. (A) Doctor.

(B) Lawyer.

(C) Plumber.

10. (A) The phone line is busy.

(B) The machine is out of paper.

(C) The plug is unplugged.